AKASHIC RECORDS

Collective Keepers of Divine Expression

LUMARI

 AMETHYST

Cover Art: Lumari

Published by
AMETHYST
c/o 7 Avenida Vista Grande, Suite B7-113
Santa Fe, New Mexico PZ [87508]

TABLE OF CONTENTS

PREFACE

The Akashic Records are a vast system of organized energy that imparts the wisdom of the ages. Many ancient texts make reference to the Akashic Records or the book of life. These texts describe it as a library or book that holds vast amounts of information about our individual lives. While this description is intriguing, I wanted to know about the system itself. In my spiritual practice and explorations, I continually discover that what appears to be simple, turns out to be richly and deliciously complex.

Deep within, I knew this to be the case of the Akashic Records, so I sought them out. I wanted a dialogue with the system itself, not for references to my own personal path, but to discover what this system is and how it works. How does the Akashic gather information? How far does it reach? Can we approach the Akashic to gain a deeper understanding of the life processes that can bring us a greater experience of the fullness of being? Can we encounter access points to connecting with our own higher aspects and the vast spiritual wisdom many of us seek? Can we find new avenues for growth and awakening in the Akashic?

It was in this context that I approached the Collective of the Akashic Records and began the wonderful conversations that became this book. The Akashic introduced themselves to me as, The Akashic Records - Collective Keepers of Divine Expression. This title or name distinguishes their group consciousness from the information that they hold. The Collective Keepers of Divine Expression are the group of beings who gather and contain the wisdom and workings of the universe. They speak as one voice. Their focus is to gather, contain and share everything that has happened and unfolded in the universe and within that, all thoughts, explorations, intentions and their actual, probable and possible results.

The Akashic Collective do not have a specific personality or emotional body. They are not especially conversational, as you or I might be. They link words and phrases together to tickle awareness and challenge thought process. This book, written with their words and phrases, may sometimes require a few read-throughs to understand their phrasing, and to assimilate the energies conveyed in their words.

This book contains selections from our conversations together. We, the Akashic and myself, created a space into which a greater comprehension of those wonderful systems could be accessed. I, as channel, provided the space, while they explained their context of being. Therefore, they are speaking to me and I am sharing our conversations with you. Sometimes, in this book, they are speaking directly to me. Other times, they are speaking directly to you. The Collective knew that

I would write and publish this book before I did. Naturally, they took the opportunity to speak to all who would read it.

In our conversations together, they were gracious in clarifying who they are, what they do and how the system of the Akashic is accessed. As I anticipated, their system and presence is deliciously complex. I was and am delighted, embraced and absorbed by their responses and their enormity. The Collective more than answered all of my inquiries. They provided expansive information to deepen our understanding of the vastness of reality and suggested many different themes and avenues of exploration within their system. They also created three simple methods to help people gain more access to the Akashic Records.

The Akashic Records is a rich, ever-changing awareness which delights in the unique and inclusive universal expressions of consciousness. In this book, "The Akashic Records - Collective Keepers of Divine Expression," the Collective share their amazing process for encompassing the fullness of life. They reveal the wisdom and understanding of their own being, so we can grow into our greater fullness. In recognition of the vast exploration of consciousness, and in dedication to the pursuit of joy, awakening, honor and freedom, I share their words with you.

Lumari

Chapter One:

INTERCONNECTED WISDOM

We are the Collective Keepers of Divine Expression known as the Akashic Records. We are a system of record keeping, unlike what exists anywhere else. On earth, people seek intelligent computers to keep records and data on specific events and the like. We are an intelligent alive system that records in a multidimensional way, all of the activities, intents and motivations of all beings, systems and events in all times; future, present and past. We carry dimensional frequencies that you, in your present human mind cannot put into words, because the experience of them is too distant for you at this time. We are a collective and individual life force and awareness that is actually rooted within your energy source.

It is important to note, that the full impetus of our creation is not known to us, since we occurred in awareness after, but anything after that moment of awareized creation we do contain. We experienced

11

our coming into being, but not that which preceded it. It occurs to us, and also you once stated (speaking to Lumari), that if a being or civilization could fully experience what they have felt and thought through their actions, they would be better equipped to make the decisions that suited them and be more fully able to take responsibility for their actions in a multi-leveled way. We were created to suit this endeavor. We are a fully aware consciousness that tracks and holds and distantly experiences the modes of all life. This seems like a huge endeavor to you. It is. But your grasp of the holography of it, is limited. We are a collective consciousness. This means that while we are singular of purpose and even of format, we are separate in task orientation and system tracking and discovery. You see, we are more than a record keeping system.

We are developed to be aware and to be in magical discovery about what we encounter in our recording of events and the like. This intrigues you, doesn't it? *Yes it does.* Well rightfully so. We not only perform specific duties, as you might call them, but also enjoy what we do, find fulfillment within it and evolve in our own right by this endeavor. This is a highly complicated system, but remember, you do not create consciousness without the impetus and capabilities of awareness, growth and fulfillment within discovery. This is a wonderful thing.

We are very lighthearted about our work. It is a combination of distance and love. We hold all beings within the grace of love that we carry and hold the records of their experiences for them, in trust, so that they may be availed of whatever they can for their growth and evolution.

We have the ability to track vibrational energy as well as the events, intents and lessons that are created within any energy form. Naturally, we most often track the awareized energy that you would call *means* consciousness and being. But we also track what you would consider pure energy that is generally without your understanding of awareness. Of course, all energy is aware, but some energy forms are much more loosely configured than others. Perhaps less self aware, perhaps not. It is more on a frequency ratio that we understand it, than in the personal and human terms.

How this works, on a general level, mind you, ~~is that~~ there is a train or a channel or a thread onto which we latch. We follow this thread for all beings. We do this all at once. We can systematically organize this thread into varied themes, events or time frames, in whatever fashion is most appropriate and understood by the individual. Naturally race memories and species memories and galactic memories are also collected and worked with in this same organizational manner. It is truly multidimensional. We work within a holographic light dimension that is without time or space. Everything occurs within the moment for us, and yet we can also work with the probable realities, the eventual realities and the simultaneous realities that are occurring in one moment of time, as you call it. We would call it a moment of focus.

Within a moment of focus, we pull a specific thread and then extract, the essential ingredients. We do not lose any information or experiences, but given the nature of our purpose, you might say we formulate a synopsis of events for each individual or situation. This synopsis is a coded container, which expands to reveal the details, thereby showing what lives individuals have lead, what was accomplished or not and what was learned, given the individual's original intent for being and choosing that life. It may appear to be organized by topic or theme, but it is not that simple.

For example, each individual has a multidimensional purpose on this planet. As an individual on planet earth, you also have a multidimensional plan in the highest of consciousness. Now, if we look at your present life on earth, we can pick up the certain areas you would want to know about, given who you are and what your purpose is in the many levels that your purpose falls under. We can then show you (again in very loose terms) what actions have been taken, the affects, and attributes of those actions, and what you have learned and experienced from those actions, for your personal growth and for your chosen work.

We can also "show" you how your actions, assessments and decisions have come about or are related to your past lives, as you would call them, other lives on other worlds and the like. This would give you a strong basis for reflection upon what your intent was, how it is going, and what changes if any you would make in this life, in probable realities that you are living within a parallel system, in probable realities that you are partially exploring but, not fully within, and many more options.

You are endeavoring to illuminate yourself and others about their access to the information already present in the universe. The Akashic Records are also likened to a library. This suggests that the information of collected events and understandings are in existence, in one place and in an accessible format. This is so. The Records are in an accessible format. You may delve into them at any time. Generally, though, an individual delves into the Records at their particular level of understanding. Generally, there is only an opening of energy to bring you a step along the way in your understanding of the nature of events, and in particular, your own personal events. This is due to the nature of our created format. While we are more open to some, we are less open to others. You see, there is a great deal of stored wisdom within our system. This means that the 'nature of discovery' is also present within us.

The nature of discovery includes: the full events, thought processes and workings of discoveries in a holistic sense. If you had developed a particular technique for working with energy, it would be contained within our format. Beings of like mind, informational growth, and also, evolutionary growth would indeed be able to access this to some degree.

All information, however it is organized within us, is safeguarded. The safe guard is the vibrational context of the individual or group who is seeking the information. Information is held within its vibrational pattern and context. Access to this information is gained by holding and maintaining the vibrational levels in which the information resides. If you or your higher self can maintain, continually, a high degree or a compatible degree of energy that relates to the format of information you are seeking, then you could, with proper understanding, access this information. In a general sense, this is why many people come up with the same invention at the same time on your planet. They are resonating at the same vibrational frequencies as the information within the Akashic Records and therefore, because their intents are similar, they access the information about the invention at the same time. Of course, some individuals resort to stealing, as in computer theft and the like. But the genuine simultaneous occurrence of like inventions or similar newer understandings of a format are due to tapping into the Akashic Records.

Each person who connects with this information will then have the opportunity to express this finding in the way that suits them. If you were an artist and had discovered a new kind of perception that led to a new visionary experience which could be translated into paint or whatever media is your preference, then it would occur in your world as an unfolding of your particular energies and talent. This new perception would manifest in the world through your form and be your style, so to speak. Later, others could or would adapt their energies to this and bring forth their own styles.

This is the same information translated into your personal way of it. It is similar to the unified field theory in physics. The ancient ones had discovered that, "as above, so below," or in other words one action (this includes thought) in one area of existence, impacts another area of existence which is a total impact to the whole. For all is specifically and undeniably related. The scientists, working in their concept of reality based on the objective theories that have been working in that realm, did not see this system as a whole. They were focused in the individual and did not really see that the impact of one atom could affect the entire universe. Therefore, when the unified field theory came about, it was a break through not only in scientific thinking, but in your understanding of reality, which tends to be splintered into spirit and science. This information and its understanding, actually was being worked on by several scientific thinkers at one time. All of them, in their own way, tapped into the Akashic Records. This does not mean that they broke in. This means that with the focus of their work, and the particular vibrations that they could maintain in their lives, they then had access to this information. It also means that the information was accessed in the ways they could best perceive and utilize it. It is an individual focus. Some scientists found that this actually correlated to the understanding of the Buddhists in years gone by. The united universe exists within the individual, even in the grain of sand. Some did not even know of this, but endeavored to find this in more specific realms within their sciences.

This is one facet of how the galactic memory, the Akashic Records, works as a library. Now, naturally we also hold interstellar and universal information as well. Interstellar and universal information could be viewed as the astronomy of events, or the history of a species evolution, or spiritual wisdom. The kind of information you gain in the more expanded area of universality, would depend on 1) your focus, 2) your personal vibration 3) your capacity and 4) your intent for accessing this kind of information. The discovery or information you receive is based on those criteria.

Now, remember, most often this way of accessing the Akashic Records for scientific information and the like is actually more like a blunder. The intent was not to access the information from us, therefore those receiving the information energetically stumbled upon it because their vibratory rates, intentions and capacities led them to the Akashic Records, to the repository of that information. Most people do not know how to access Akashic information. Those who do stumble upon it, maintain a field of energy that is compatible with a specific access of information and so they receive further input in this area.

You could intend to receive information from the Records themselves. This is a more direct route. Some people in more spiritual alignment do ask for this information. We do respond to this. Again, it is within the context of their personal vibration that we respond. You will not get the wisdom of the universe showered upon you if you cannot contain and resonate to that vibration. Our creator made sure of this for everyone's protection. This includes the seeker. You could blow up or go mad with information that is not appropriate to your vibrational energy. This is serious, although we are lighthearted about this. And still, it does happen that events in a person's life throw them into another energetic state that is not compatible with the information that they have already received, based on their previous energetic vibration. Your mental health institutions are filled with these people.

Now, to gain access is to ask. To receive access is to be open. The expression of this access is ill-defined. This means that you do not get the formula inserted into your brain when you ask for it. It filters into your system and you perceive something other than what was previously present. Sometimes this can be a flash of insight. Or perhaps, a chill or goose-bumps, in affirmation of a query. Sometimes the process is slower and cannot be thought of as instantaneous at all. It appears to be a series of events that leads to the discovery. It is all the same to us. We are not attached to how you receive your requested information. We use the terms that you understand. Even the term "information" is a weak description of a holistic viewing of reality in simultaneous time and space.

When you enter, or have access to the Akashic Records you enter into a holographic environment in which there is access to certain information based on your intent and vibration. Again, it is a matter of tuning. You could call us the tree of knowledge, for within us is contained all of the information and wisdom that has been recorded, as far as we know. This means that from the initial inception of our creation, we have collected a vast amount of information into which all civilizations, intelligences and expressions of being are assimilated.

These terms, 'stored,' 'information' and even 'collected' are weak descriptions of the true nature of wisdom. Information is a static event. There is only so much information, and in and of itself, information does nothing. It is inert matter, as you would term it. It is a collection of notations about something. It cannot, in and of itself, impart any wisdom. The letters of a word, mean nothing unless the full energy of that word, its concept and living energy is present within it. Now, that is what a computer is like, or any format of information. It is then up to each individual's perception to bring life to the information and translate it into wisdom.

Within our system, what you would call information is "awareized." This means that the emotion, the insight, the tonality, the frequency and the awareness is within the information. A word or term describing this state does not exist in your language. There is a term called the living word, that may describe it better. But information, wisdom and experience are not stored in words. We and the information are awareized. We are living beings who contain this awareized information. We are separate from the information we contain. We have not lived it. We hold it. The Akashic Records are not a static repository. We are a growing, expanding dynamic system of being and wisdom united in participation.

From our viewpoint, it is hard to describe what the experience of entry into the Akashic is for an individual. Naturally you will receive the best explanation that we can describe.

When a being enters the Akashic Records, their personal frequency triggers certain responses from us. This is that their frequency opens certain doorways into the living information that is contained within us. This trigger then opens, or not, certain living information to be experienced. Many people see or feel this within the near death experience. They enter the blessing of the Akashic Records and what is revealed to them is their full life experience. We are not the ones who tell people to stay in the energy field that you call death or to return to your home world. We hold the experience of a life time of living on earth for the individual. We reveal this lifetime experience to the individual, in a manner that is specifically and individually appropriate. This is the passage gateway. In order for you to understand what you have accomplished and what your intent was in this lifetime, you are availed of this particular view point that we share with you. Your life passes before you. The passage through the tunnel of light is often a signal of the death experience for humans and some other beings. Not all beings experience this format.

To continue, a consciousness of your kind needs the signal to return and it follows this tunnel to our entry point. This is a particular area, you would call it, where the human's information about his or her experience is stored. There really is no area and there really is no storage, but this is a way to describe it for you to better understand. Then, in this state of mind and being, a person will grasp what he or she can and go somewhere else. Again, even the word somewhere is misleading. But, our concept of reality is very different. For us there is no space, there is no where or here, and there is no time. It is all within the focus of awareness.

In other experiences of us, one is entering a different portal. This is not access to a full life experience per se, but into the awareized information that is in tune with a person's frequency, or rate and quality of vibration. So one will have access to only certain information in order to retrieve and experience this formatted knowledge. This formatted information then vibrates as a homing frequency to the individual and a collective relationship is formed. Within that vibrational relationship the individual will open the gates and be opened himself to the sought after information.

Now all of the information is given at once. For example, if you remember the story of Einstein, he had a flash of insight while he was doing his mundane routines, and there after created the theory of relativity. He had been working on this for some time. His frequency was raised to a particular level into which he could maintain that frequency and then enter the awareized information format that was evading him. He did not receive all of the information that was available within that subject. He received or encountered the information that he could work with at that time. Later, he did receive further information, but certain things evaded him for several reasons. One reason is that he could not contain or hold the frequency of the other levels of that informational expression. Another reason is that within that further information, the frequency of humanity would negate its understanding or use it inefficiently.

There are certain lock out systems that are in place. In the Akashic Records these lockout systems protect those seeking information beyond their capacity and also those who may use the information for ill-intent. This does not mean that information can never be used for ill informed intents. It means that given a particular understanding of frequency, the planetary system will actually block the frequency from being received. Access to the Akashic Records and to that specific information would be denied. The frequency of the planet, herself, would block certain frequencies, and the humans of the planet would block others from being received. For example, if the information of the unified field were received during a war, certain devious military personnel would try to use that to their advantage. Then they could conceivably destroy far more than they intend. Now, we appreciate the curiosity of beings to explore and discover their universe in their own ways. But within your system, many people do not own responsibility for their actions in a full understanding of those same actions. They do not have the scope of the repercussions of their actions. In their immediacy and zeal to discover or invent or solve, they, generally, do not care what happens later or what the results for the future may be as they are seized with the emotion of their intent and discovery. Attention to their immediate intentions tends to supercede their long term vision or responsibility.

These are some of the blocking systems that are within us to help insure that certain information is received, worked with and understood before more information is gained. After all, you cannot learn algebra if you have no concept of the numbers and what they can do. This goes for all frequencies, all systems and all beings. Humans are no exception to the rule. No being has access to information beyond their vibrational rate or their frequency. And also we have learned from experiences, that many forms of trickery are used to access inappropriate information.

There is no system ever created that insures particular events and responsibilities. There is no specifically predetermined, pre-programmed, singular outcome or result generated by accessing information at a given time. This insurance policy, that some people seek, would be a closed system of creation. There are no closed systems in that regard. There are systems that have lock outs until the particular evolutionary vibration is reached, but the system itself is not really closed, it is locked. Closed means that there is no access and never any access to that system at all. Locked means that specific criteria are necessary to gain access. The universe is an open system, which has specific vibratory criteria for access to certain wisdoms and experiences.

Another thing to note: We, the Akashic Records, do not control what any being does with the information once it is received. That is not our job, so to speak. We are simply and complexly a system of awareized information that can be accessed. So what you do with the information once it is received is your responsibility. You are held accountable for this responsibility. We are not the judge in this. That is for others. We are the system of living information. Using poor Einstein again, if he knew that this atomic information would be the cause of major destruction in the past and as yet the possibility to come, perhaps he would have discovered it and then destroyed that information. Perhaps he would not have encouraged its use. In his present state of being, Einstein is working with his responsibilities within the formatting of the information he accessed, what it created and how it was and is used. We do know that no being can understand all of the ramifications of their wisdom. This is understood. Yet, many throw caution to the winds and go forward when they do indeed know that what will or is most likely to occur will have negative results in certain areas. There is full responsibility in this matter. You have full responsibility for all of your actions. This does not mean that you will rot in hell for your work. It means that you will be held accountable for those actions and then be given opportunities to solve those very actions, whether it is within the same living time frame you call a lifetime sequence, or in another lifetime sequence or in other ways.

The being and the created situation, is always given the opportunity for the recognition of responsibility, the possibility for full understanding and the opportunities for resolution. In this, we also play a part. For, not only are the actions you have taken, the thoughts and decisions you have made and the intensions and purposes of those actions held within the Akashic body, but the future opportunities for responsibility and resolution are also present. All of this and more is contained within our system. So you would say, we have much within us.

Chapter Two:

SHARING THE TRUST

We have all sorts of information. We are a travel agent. We have all planetary systems annotated within our system. We know where they are, who is upon them, what their evolutionary state is, their frequency, their intent, and also their climate, orbitational information and the like. We would hold the temperatures and changes that are occurring within each and every system, as well as the events of the civilizations, the people, the other growing beings and all of the pertinent information. We are also monitored, as you would call it, by a few very worthy beings who have access to the full of us. So, if you are a being who is an explorer, and have the intent to explore other systems, you might come to the Akashic Records for that information. You send a letter to PO box..... Just kidding. We are lighthearted beings, after all. You would have a particular vibratory rate that would receive certain information about the systems that would be opened to your energies and then proceed from there. Please note that this interplanetary information is closed to your human endeavors. You, as a race of beings, are not evolved enough for this form of travel and encounter. You need to experience those who have traveled to your world, before you travel to others. But, others do this on a continual basis.

Again, not all beings have the framework of responsibility firmly within them. Also, while an explorer may have this responsibility within him or her, the next level of informational sharing may not. An individual or group of individuals may have a specific understanding and wisdom that generates a very high level of responsibility, and yet their peers or progeny may not appreciate that same level of knowing.

As an example, a grandfather may understand the full impact of a handgun, because he used it in combat in war and it saved his life and the lives of his fellows. He may think it is an appropriate weapon to engage in, within a war framework. He realizes what occurred in his life and in the greater framework of your world. He understands his responsibilities in this matter. His son, may have a different understanding. Perhaps he has heard the stories of how this gun saved his father's life. He heard how his father was a hero. He respects the weapon and it's capacities to protect and to harm. His father taught him about the care and responsibilities of the gun. The son uses the gun for sport or hunting. He has his responsibilities within his actions. He is careful in its use. He locks it away to protect others from harm. He remembers the stories of his father and knows how dangerous this weapon is and how responsible he must be in its use. Now, the gun progresses to the grandson. He may not understand the nature of his actions. He has not experienced the need of a gun in war. He has nothing to defend. He was not trained in the code of honor for a soldier. He was taught by his father, who used the gun for hunting. Yet there isn't any hunting in their area. The gun is now a symbol. It doesn't have a specific use, for protection or for hunting game. The grandson has a different understanding about guns. He has watched a lot of television and movies. His ideas about guns may be objects of power. He might imagine it used in many other circumstances that neither the father nor grandfather would think were appropriate. The grandson, could use it to kill indiscriminately, simply because he does not feel the same level of responsibility or have the same level of wisdom as either his father or his grandfather.

Information does not create negative results. It is the use of information by those responsible for the information that can cause negative results. In this example, guns already existed. No one in this example created them. Yet, by using the gun, each person had their own relationship with the gun. The gun is a source of experience and information. A negative result is not caused by having information about the guns. Its misuse is the responsibility of the grandson and others like him. We are not advocating guns. We are not advocating firearms, war training or the like. We use this example to show how information becomes a tool of whoever wants to use it, when it is available to them. This does not mean that the information was inappropriately given. It means it was inappropriately used. In its original format it was appropriate. Then you might say it degenerated. Therefore, an individual can access information from the Akashic Records, and be in complete and responsible resonance with that information and its use. Yet, other people or other uses can make that information harmful or dangerous. If the first individual had concerns that by retrieving this information it may fall 'into the wrong hands' and cause harm, and this individual retrieved the information anyway, then some responsibility for the future harm would lie with them. If they had no idea that this type of harm could or would ensue, then the responsibility of the harm rests solely in the individual actions.

Now, we use this previous example for travelers as well. When the other planetary beings, who have been on your planet many times, arrived on your world, with the information they received, they did not have the intent to create harm here. Yet, as time went on, others came with different intents, and a whole series of events occurred within that endeavor. The explorers are not to blame in this. For they did not have an ill-intent towards the beauty of this world. Yet, their progeny or their loose associations, did not share the same views and did not hold this living planet being as sacred. Therefore their actions did cause harm. Things like this do occur in all systems and when it does, those beings are held accountable for their actions. This means they are responsible until some form of specific resolution can be grasped. The resolution is also their responsibility. This resounds on the energetic levels as well as in whatever system it occurs, and by using earth as an example, the resolution would also take place on a physical level.

We explain the importance of personal responsibility for the information and access to the Akashic Records because, you are seekers of your own paths to spirit. You may want to know something of your own personal path, whether in this life or past lives. You may also want to explore other philosophies, methods or discoveries that may help humanity. You are and will be responsible for whatever you learn. Knowing this will help you choose which path of actions you take. Your vibrational compatibility may grant you entrance to information. Your personal integrity and foresight will determine how you use it.

In a certain way, you can get into the Akashic Records on your own at any time, but it generally does not work in that way. A being would need to be consistently aware of the Records in order to delve into them at any time they wished. This is not usually the case. One is focused on one's particular life time and experience and therefore work within that focus. It would generally be counter productive to continually check into the Records of one's own life for verification of events and information. This would be like looking up the previous answers to particular questions all of the time, and then basing the next series of actions upon those findings. Generally speaking each event or each decision has its own particular merits and pathways to discovery. So, if you are within a certain event and want to check to make sure you are doing the right thing, conferring with the Akashic Records would not be the best way to do that. You all have at your disposal many psychics who can help you in that type of situation. Some of them do indeed check into the Akashic Records in a vague way. But many of them tend to open up to the fuller experience of the being they are reading and then bring forth that information. You are all on the pathway of wisdom and clarity, and the answers will unfold for you.

There are also different systems of information available that are not specifically related to the Records. We are aware of them, and naturally contain them within us. In the manner that we work, it is not our place to give you that information. Your innate sense of discovery and truth will lead you to your own understandings and wisdom.

Now, there are appropriate ways to use the Records for your benefit in a sporadic way of inquiry. One way to explore the Records for personal growth is by recognizing and following patterns of experience. As an example, perhaps there is a situation wherein the individual has already had several events with similarities that he or she is working out in this lifetime. Perhaps a business arrangement is being discussed that seems to have similarities with a previous business endeavor that did not work out particularly well. Yet, while this one seems very different on the surface, there is a hint of a similarity that does not feel right. By connecting with the highest within yourself, and also intending to encounter the Akashic Records on the previous matter of business, one can gain great insight into that new situation that is unfolding. It does not mean that one would receive the information about how to proceed and the nature of the future events. One may, however be able to connect with the underlying currents and patterns in the personal life that have led up to the previous event and from there notice the fuller similarities of this event in question.

An example of this: a man is engaged in a new business endeavor. He has had previous experience with business before and it was not to his liking. The activities of the business were fine, but the relationships and the agreements between the people were breached and this made for a difficult time for him. Now, a new situation presents itself. It has all of the elements that he wishes. Yet, there is something about this that gives him cause to question whether this is right for him or not. Agreements are underway, and yet something within this has a familiar feel of doom to him. In this instance, he may wish to come into contact with the Records, and review the scenes from the previous business endeavor. Perhaps the lessons from the other business experience were not fully learned. Perhaps he was naive in thinking that he could make a system work that was not to his liking. Perhaps he has difficulties with particular personalities. Perhaps these personalities are similar in underlying traits to his parents who were not supportive of him. Perhaps the methods being employed in this are against his fuller nature and he is seduced by the possibility of working in this field, but has not fully understood that he is giving up his truth in order to do this. Perhaps he is one who does not like to compromise in matters and is setting up yet another business deal in which it is all about compromise. There are a few underlying patterns that could be applicable to this man's situation. By viewing the Akashic Records, he could explore the past business endeavors and relationships and discover what he was to learn from those events. If he is clear enough to do this, then he could intend to learn those lessons without the struggle in the new business.

If it were due to his working with unsavory personalities in order to do what he wants in the world, this could be discovered in the past experience. If it were due to the relationship with his parents that could be revealed within the Records and he could more fully embrace this experience and heal whatever needed to be healed. If it is about compromise, he could see where within himself he is unwilling to compromise and follow that into himself where he could uncover this pattern and resolve it. This is how one could approach the Records for further information about present circumstances.

If one was interested in some past life information, one could also explore the Akashic Records for specific events or lessons within those areas. There is a thread that needs to be followed within all of the approaches. One needs to be in harmony with the events one is checking. If you are not ready for that information, in almost all cases it is not given. This means that just because you are working out issues of leadership, you will not uncover all of the lifetimes that you were a ruler and whatever breaches of power you had done. You may, on the other hand, encounter one phase of a particular lifetime that has a message for you and that will further your understanding of the events you are working on. This is how it generally works. There are individuals who can access all of the information in the records about themselves. But this is highly unusual, and extremely rare for individuals of earth. Most often this happens in other systems of highly evolved beings who already have understanding of their full scope of life's expression and are looking for in depth clarification that can occur in a simultaneous way for them.

There are those beings on your planet who do reach the Records on a more regular basis, and continually discover events of their past lives and present lives that give them clues as to where they are in uncovering the underlying thrust of their natures and the events that stem out of their natures, which you call experiences. They are not always aware that they are in the Records themselves, but they are helped by this action, and their inner self knows how to travel to receive the information that is appropriate to them at that time. Again, it is done by vibrational frequency, so if the frequency and the tone of the frequency and the strength and duration of the frequency is compatible with the information sought, then this information is imparted. What the person does with this information is his or her responsibility. They could easily learn from this information and open to new avenues of expression in their lives, which would open the gateways within them for a greater understanding of their personal intent. In this they could thereby learn from those experiences in a fuller manner. They could also just be amused by the information and not do anything about it. There are many responses to the information and many other ways to get similar information than to approach the Records for it. But contained within us is also the impetus towards the events. This is not always clear in the other manners of expression for information.

Let us speak about going into the Records for another person's experiences. This is also a more unusual situation. There are beings who can do this, given their vibration and frequency and the fuller scope of qualifications to enter the Records. They would encompass a wider expression of form than is generally seen within humans. There are beings from other worlds who can do this more readily. Remember, you are a young race of beings. You have not evolved to the point in time where you have such a great access. Generally, it would not serve you at this time. But it is possible and some humans so this.

For this access, usually there is an inward permission given by the person who is having their personal lives revealed. This is a full permission to have revealed what is being discussed at the time. One cannot, from your point of view, go into anyone's lifetime, and crack the Records about them to find out what you want to know. But, if the person is also seeking this information and gives permission in an inward way and without coercion, then information is given, while taking into account the vibrations of both people. Therefore, one may have full permission and still not have access due to vibration and personal intent.

So, in this way, one cannot hypnotize an individual, and receive permission to enter the Records and acquire information. The intent would be off, the agreement would be coerced and the vibration would not resonate properly for this endeavor to take place. It is important to note, that intent is not a one moment thought. As we view intent, it is a deep vibrational current held within your personal system. It is not a momentary thought or well constructed idea held in order to get something or receive something. You can not intend something in the moment that gives you entrance to the Akashic Records and then later return to your original frame of mind. You cannot change your vibration for a short period of time, with a mal-intent and gain access to information about someone else. This can easily be discerned. One would be required to have a sustained intent beyond the immediate time frame, a vibrational resonance that has been sustained and clarified for a period of time and the full inner and outer agreement of the individual for access. This also includes the same criteria of the individual whose information you are seeking. It has to be within all parties best interest for this to be revealed in this manner. There is more to this configuration, but you have the understanding of how it would work in general terms.

Chapter Three:

BLESSED INFUSION

You have seen a bit on how we work. We have explained the systems for you. We would also like to share how the system works in each individual.

There is an opening in each individual that is likened to a thread or the opening for a thread to be present. It is an energetic form that is present within each individual. Within this is a bond with us. It is with this that you travel to meet the Records. The Records to not live within you as other systems do. Your brain carries activities to other systems. Your heart is aligned with other systems. Many of your body parts have counterparts in the etheric realm. This means that the vibrations of the physical organs have a system set up which is also etheric. Certain systems of knowledge actually reside within the organs and their etherics. The Records are beyond that. We do not reside within you, we are beyond you, in descriptive terms.

When you learn of the fuller heart chakra, when you access its true location and frequency, you will realize that this is a system of travel for many beings outside of the human realm of existence. This travel system resides within you. It is activated by many components within your physical and energetic form. It can be accessed by the physical and also by the energetic. It is very distinct from the solar plexus. It is the diaphragm area, the center of integration within your form. Now, within this is actually the energetic format as well. This relates to your being in very real sense. It is similar to an energetic chord that, when sent outwards gives you access to the heart travel energies. This is a particular format of travel. When one travels through this fuller heart center, the greater experience of love and its realms opens to you. Fullness, healing and a great sense of peace is present. One still travels, meaning that one can experience other dimensions and spatial formats, but it is seated within this vibration.

With the Records, we are not located within your system at all. We are availed of your system and you are availed of ours, but we, in fact, remain separate from you in a real and particular sense. It is not that you do not have access to us, but the Akashic Records are not located within your form, or for that matter within any personal form at all. We could say that we are completely separate, but that might be misleading for you. This frame of separation is more of ownership. Nothing is ever separated from the Source of All. Yet, the individuation of events and realms is in fact a form of separation. It is a vibrational separation that limits the focus and access until one is ready for it. Which, of course, means that one would have access when one could hold the vibration of that sphere. It does not mean it is unavailable. Many beings, humans included, travel to realms that are not fully established vibrations within them. Note though, that this is accomplished by guidance and help, and not by the full volition, intent and vibration of the individual. So, too, with us, there are beings who can gracefully enter us, and consider it a great wonder. Yet, we do not reside within them, they approach the possibility of residing within us for a time.

This is accomplished in the vibrational realms and includes the energies of the individual being within ourselves. No one actually resides within us as beings, but as you can reside within the heart of the universe, then this is possible. We would be considered a space and a time and a location by your standards of expression, but this does not describe us as we see ourselves in the broader sense. We are a distinct consciousness that holds and transmits the awareized information of consciousness. All consciousness has connections to us, and their intents, vibrations and wisdom is contained within us as an ever flowing living presence. It changes as they change. It learns as they learn. It evolves as they evolve, and yet, the recording, the notation, the presence and reality of the totality of it exists within us. In a moment of time, the universe unfolds you to us and we in turn can do this for you when you connect to us. It is as though you broadcast your every thought and activity and intent to us and we hold it for you and for the universal energies of consciousness. Higher beings, in the vibrational sense, can have access to your individual and race progress. They do not need to travel to earth and visit. Most care not to. Some do visit and even incarnate to have a greater understanding of your process of evolution and to find new ways to help you all in this growth stage. This growth stage you are in is very important. It is an opportunity for you all to know the fuller meaning of reality and the Divine within yourselves and within the universe. It is also an opportunity for other beings to share in this process and perhaps to help you make the leap towards your understanding of the greater divinity within.

This can be a very exciting time for many. It is another wake up call in your world. There have been many wake up calls for humans. There are with all beings. While many beings in particular civilizations have within them the fullest expression of intent towards evolution within the energies of the Divine, often times a period of intensity is required to gently or not so gently push the individuals and the civilization towards a fuller expression. Some individuals naturally have their own impetus and this varies in expression, dedication and intensity within each individual. This is the same for races and civilizations of beings. When it is deemed necessary, an influx of energy is exerted, which coincides with the time for evolutionary growth. Earth is in this framework at this time.

This was decided long ago, and a particular time frame was set for this to occur. It coincides with the planetary evolutionary possibility. Possibility means that there is the opportunity for this evolution to occur. It does not mean that a particular outcome is inevitable. There are many possibilities and many outcomes that can be experienced. It is your opportunity as individuals and as a race to encounter the divinity within and to embrace your fullness. This includes responsibility for your actions.

The decision to engage this influx of energy at this time, was foreseen many years ago. It has been told of in your ancient literature. It is timed with planetary movement in your sector of the galaxy and compliments the planetary activities of other systems. This is a holistic approach towards evolution which is what evolution is. Evolution is holistic. One does not genuinely evolve in a scientific mode. One evolves in a full realm of areas within the individual and the race. One cannot look at the scientific advances of a race of beings and conclude that they are evolved. One can conclude that they are scientifically advanced within that particular focus. There is a galactic dilemma when the scientific advances of a civilization exceeds the race's abilities - when science and technology exceeds responsibility towards life, relatedness, compassion, growth and divinity. There is a lack or flaw within that course of events. There is something missing within that focus.

Intent towards growth in a personal and racial format is not necessarily present within your world. The understanding that what one does to one life is done to all life, is not yet understood. There is a lack in responsiveness towards all of life. This has been present in most civilizations of your world. This is altering a bit, but the question for you all, is, "is it altering enough to change your future into one of caring, understanding, harmony, responsibility and respect for all of life as divine expressions of the universal source?" The potential for this to occur is great. Also, it is balanced by the potential in the opposite direction, your world is more focused on the polarities of nature and not on the whole of it. Can you see this as individuals? If you can see this as individuals, can you initiate the changes within yourselves that will embrace this new format on earth?

It remains to be seen. You are capable of this change. You are to know that you are capable of this change. Otherwise the opportunity would not present itself. Many of you hold great keys to this unfoldment within yourselves. In truth, it is not enough to hold the frequencies for evolution. Even though you can gain access to miraculous energies of blessing and light, it does not mean that you are increasing the evolution of humanity. There is more to this grand event than frequency. There is dedication, truth, responsibility and honor. A frequency, no matter how refined, cannot and will not impart this grace and wisdom to you. You may access it, but just like the information within the Akashic Records, what you do with it, how it unfolds within your lives and the lives of others is your responsibility. This is a truth. You are responsible. This responsibility is a blessing. You hold this blessed evolution into harmony, joy, freedom and grace within your own being. The exploration of Divine frequency is just one facet of evolution.

Many of you are uncovering the myths that were realities and created your world. Many of them are not so pleasant to remember. Many of you have been exceedingly brutal in your incarnations. Can you take ownership of your brutality and embrace the fears that created it so that you can open yourself to the forgiveness which is within the divinity itself? Can you follow the threads and weave a new cloth?

There are beings here, now, on your planet that are from different worlds than earth. There are humans who are born of the flesh who are not human. They are time travelers who know what is going on here and have chosen through great obstacles to come here and to help you to change the frequency of your lives and this planet. They have had to encounter the limitation of forms, of systems and events, sometimes for lifetimes, on this planet, just to help you in this moment of time. They have had to lose memory and associations to fully engage on this world to access much for the All. You may very well know some of these people. They are working with the Divine frequencies and they are helping you to alter the evolution to your highest blessings. Many of this group are actually rather obscure. Most are not well known. There are those chosen to lead many people. They are considered teachers, gurus, spiritual leaders and they come in all races. These leaders are very few in number. Follow your inner truth to discover who lives by the word and frequency and responsibility of their being.

There are many more who are relatively unknown. They come into your life to reveal certain truths and leave you to discover your path. While this is difficult for them on the human level, in their greater selves, they are in joy. They hold many more secrets than you may know. They have different tasks. Some work for humanity. Some work with humanity, but their focus is on the galactic whole. Some work on this planet to accelerate specific frequencies and gateways which resonate with systems very far removed from any human experience. Some work with the planet, Herself, and everything else takes a lesser role.

Please know that this planet will live her life with or without you. She will survive and evolve and flourish with or without you. We are not predicting doom and destruction. We state a simple fact. It is your opportunity to live on this glorious planet and evolve with her. It is Her time now. It is also your time now. She, the planet, would love for you to be here, if you can hold the frequencies of Her energy and grow within your divinity. She would naturally provide you with the beauty and nourishment that is her bounty. This is your choice. This is what is considered your responsibility. You can choose at any moment. You can choose the grace and beauty of your evolution. You can choose to participate in the highest manner with the evolution of this planet and all beings on it and within it who make the choice for evolution. The question is, will you choose now?

This is the eternal now, from which you all spring and into which you may one day disappear, if it is your path to do so. Not all beings disappear into the oneness. It is not fully necessary. Then again, some beings are definitely recycled, due to many considerations. This is basically what is occurring on this world at this time. The balance of your lives is all up to you. You can choose at any moment for your full evolution. Some beings have already done this. Some beings think that they have, but in truth, they have not. Others do not even know that this is what is going on. Where do you stand within this? We channel through Lumari to speak with you. Much of this she indeed already knows, and is being gracious enough to avail us of her energies to speak with you. We are honored to do this and honored by her gift of this opportunity for us to speak. Normally, we do not speak to the beings of earth. We are not approached in this manner and many cannot hold this fuller expression of our frequency.

This is your time. This is your eternal now. So, we ask you to choose the path of your evolution, right now. Make your choice and be present to the opportunities that this choice will unveil. The results of your choice will unfold in your life, your world and the universal.

W e will begin to discuss how we gather our information. Everything links up with the Akashic Records. This link up is a frequency that each being and circumstance sends out which triggers a response from us, and we then collect the informational experiences that are occurring. This is a very basic way of expressing what we do. You cannot turn on and off this frequency. It is not the same frequency of entry that you would initiate to enter the Records. It is your own personal frequency that is continually radiated and triggers a response from us. Now, this may occur to you as a system within time. It is not. It is a mode of being for all beings of awareized consciousness.

All beings transmit the frequency of intent, thought and experiential expression into the universe as a whole. We are the recipients of this particular frequency. We hold this frequency for you as individuals. We hold it for you to review and to engage your growth in evolutionary terms. It is also held for others of higher vibrational evolution, to have access which is appropriate to them, to view the occurrences of individuals and races and civilizations and galactic sectors in order to more fully understand the nature of events and growth in those focuses.

As an example, imagine a being who is fully advanced in consciousness. This being not only has the capabilities to create a world, but understands the full responsibility in doing so. Many beings can create on this scale, but few understand their responsibilities in this area. So this being exists. She also has access to the particular Akashic Records of civilizations of beings in order to more fully understand the particular focus of these life forms. Now, this is all accessed with a frequency of the highest intent. There is no need for manipulation or power over others and this is seen clearly by what is being transmitted by the being of whom we speak. Therefore, having gone through the Akashic screening system and having been found acceptable for this informational access, the being is allowed to partake of this information within the specific guidelines that we set up.

Now, this being can view your world. She can see the fullness of your past evolution on this planet from creation to the present moment. She can tune in to particular individuals who are the ones who are holding an energy that is important for the being to watch. Perhaps this energy is one that holds the highest vibrations on the planet that are contained within the individuals. Perhaps it is a focus of beings with the fullest intent, who have not yet reached the highest vibration. Perhaps it is the focus on beings who are disruptive in the evolutionary process. It will be dependent on the intent and understanding of the being who is accessing the information. Perhaps this being is going to visit the planet and reach out to individuals who will have the greatest impact on the evolution of the civilization. Perhaps this being is simply monitoring the events for further understanding of the nature of humans or of the growth of the planet. This focus and intent can vary widely. We are giving you some of the manyfold examples of who would have access and the reasons for this access.

It is important to note, that we do not give access to beings in order to manipulate the events of your world or any others. This is why the intent of the being or civilization is screened. We also are evolving in this area and continually explore new ways to interpret the information we are receiving and the intent of the beings who are seeking access. Also to note, if a being is interested in manipulating the events of beings of another world for their own purposes, we are not the channel that they seek for information. We are too difficult to enter. They would seek an easier method for their information. Just as in your world, the corrupt find corrupt ways of getting what they seek. We also hold this information as well. We would know the intent of the individual, and also the parties with whom they engaged. This, for us, is just how we are.

There is no malice or retribution on our parts for any actions. We are witnesses and teachers in all events and systems. That is part of our design. We witness the expression of the Divine in all of its attributes and focuses. We honor this unfolding Divinity and contain it for those who wish to explore the elegance of the All. We share this information appropriately, and therefore, consider ourselves teachers, as well. We are aware beings who are in a collective energy framework. We are as the cells of your bodies. We are working together, aware of our individual natures and propensities and working in complete harmony within our focus. We are evolving as are all life forms. We are aware of our intents towards our personal and collective evolution and vibrational transitions. We chart ourselves as effectively as we chart all of life systems everywhere. This is our prime goal. To continually grow within ourselves and hold that evolution and chart the courses of life within all systems. We hold this energy in the greatest of heart spaces and live within the joyful expression of all beings. We do not need to agree or follow any path that is not in our highest evolutionary pattern. We thrive in this. We celebrate in this. We dance in this Divine expression of the Prime Source of which we are part and it is wonderful for us. You could say that we love our work. It is who we are and then again we are more than our work. That is the same for you.

There are more ways within the evolutionary growth events than can possibly be described. We cannot even count them, although we keep track of them all, and all of their possible twists and turns and new developments. We do this all simultaneously, in the moment, which is the ever present reality of existence, into which we become more of who we are, in an ever expanding focus. We want you to understand this so that you can be clearer in your path. We also wish to express the nature of the Akashic Records so that many of you stop thinking of us as a very large book that documents only specific events in time. Hardly. We encompass the nature of reality, its open ended possibilities, probabilities and all events in time.

An event is an occurrence. An occurrence is anything that is emitted as a vibration and any change in that vibration. Given that all things send out vibrations and also create changes in vibrational messages, your imaginations can begin to fathom the scope of our natures. This means that thought sends out vibrations. Emotion sends out vibration. Action sends out vibration. Being in and of itself sends out vibration. And all vibrations have a cause and effect relationship which also sends out vibration. Within this is a possibility factor. This means that there are also possibilities within this vibrational transmission and changing transmission that open up various options that may occur. A possibility is anything that can happen within a particular circumstance. These possibilities and options are not usually followed, but they do exist.

There is also a probability factor. A probability is a change in direction, a fork in the road if you will. This is a branching out and an experience by the individual or group of individuals which takes both highways and lives them out. So within each choice of events that occurs, there is the section that you follow within your particular ordinary focus, and there is the probable reality of another choice that could have been made, and a part of your focus actually lives out this reality as well.

This most often occurs in major life changing choices. Yet, while the fuller part of the individual is focused on the main choice, a portion of that life essence follows the other route to its probable conclusion. Sometimes these actually meet up in a reuniting event that would have been expressed and decided upon in either course of choices. Other times the focus continues into new directions. This is all experienced within the specific intent of the individual being. We follow all of that as well, and many more threads of awareness that are yet to be discovered by the human field of attention.

We consider all of these factors and hold them in our awareness. As some beings look to us for predictive information, the actual course or results of an individual's actions are what they notice. The probabilities and possibilities are not specifically revealed.

Chapter Four:

SOUNDING THE TONE

W e have spoken about entry into our system and the basics of beings who seek entry. The key for us is in the intention of the being and the vibrational frequency, its resonance, duration and quality. The frequency resonance is likened to the tone produced by the individual or collective seeking entrance or access. This would be a transmitted tone from the being to us, which we then would decipher. We would know the understanding and the wisdom and the needs of the individual by the tone of the vibrational frequency resonance. The duration of the tone emitted, is the sustained energy within that frequency. The sustained energy shows how long this vibration has been held by the individual. We decipher the intentions, quality, resonance and duration of the vibrational frequency from the individual emitting the tone. Of course we still maintain the illusion of time, but we decipher it in a very different way.

While you would look at the sequence of it, traveling in time, we would say that it is more akin to the length of it in spatial terms. This really is not how it works, but we are endeavoring to express this, without the confines of your perception of time as a sequence of events stretched in hours, days, months and years. We can decipher how long the vibrational wave is and the ability of the individual working with this tone. This is communicated within the tone itself. We also decipher the sustainability, the strength of the tone and the ability of the individual to hold the energy of the vibration that is being emitted. We then work with the quality of the tone. Is it clear? Does it waver? If it does waver, is the lowest point of the frequency able to hold the energy that is sought to be accessed? Is the tone emitted from the individual fully compatible energy and in harmony with intent and maintainability, or is it a strain on the individual and not yet fully integrated within this particular being.

These are some of the parameters that we use in deciphering the appropriateness of the information that is sought and the compatibility of the individual seeking. This is an explanation of the mechanisms which we tune into to further understand and decide whether the individual seeking access can fully handle integrating the information being sought.

We do not overload a being with information just because it is his to access, if he or she cannot hold the information within a system of integration. We do not impart information that would be discordant to the individual. At times, the information becomes discordant due to a change in the frequency of the being. This can happen at any time and through a myriad of outer and inner circumstances. We endeavor to clear all of this ahead of time.

We do not look into what you would call the future in order to see if this would work. This would be inappropriate to the endeavor of the free will of the individual and our discernment process. We could access the future in this, but the future is also a changing, evolving presence. Its unfoldment is in the range of infinite probabilities and infinite possibilities. It can be changed by any and all insights of the individual in the present, even though one particular future is already accomplished. This is also why in your world at this time, there are many who see the doom of humanity and many who see the evolution of humanity. They are all futures which do indeed exist, but in another context, they are probable futures which are yet to be enacted. In this way, you all are fully free to make choices in the moment which will alter the future and your experience of it. You may even have a split of realities into which one segment of humanity in one probable future is destroyed, while another split creates the evolution that you seek. In this way, it would not serve us or the individual to make a decision based on a future that has in one system already occurred and yet in another context has yet to unfold.

Therefore we would not give information about your future life, if you have not yet experienced it. This means that if you have indeed lived within the future here and you are already a time traveler come to earth for particular purposes, then perhaps this information could be accessed given the parameters we have already mentioned. In another instance, if you have not understood that within yourself and are not a time traveler, then your future, even if it is already revealed to us in a format that is actualized probability, would not be accessible information. So if you wanted to ask if you were getting married in the future or if you were going to die a violent death or discover a cure for AIDS, we would not give forth this information. It would not be in your best interest and it would alter your personal evolution based on the information you accessed. You would trust this information and use it as a guideline for future events, based on the fact that the future has already been revealed. This does not give you freedom of choice to alter your life and experience life within your best decisions based on your own information and evolution at the time.

Again you still have many options for access. We are not overloaded with petitions for access. You can petition for access at any time. We decide whether the access is warranted and if so, how much information is warranted. But, you can certainly ask or intend the access to the records. If you do not receive access to the information you seek, then there are other avenues to explore. This means that we have not given access, and yet as discussed previously, you have access to individuals that can help you. It is naturally dependent on what information you are seeking. Many psychics deal with the immediate questions of concern to humans. They deal with what is likely to occur next and you can figure out what to do based of these assumptions. You can go to a psychic and ask for information about your life, your job, your car and family relations. This is the easiest tack to take. There are some psychics who can uncover life purposes and the threads that you are working with at this time and also have carried over from other lifetimes. This avenue may be easier for you to receive to information you want. There are even some psychics who can work with you to alter the probable future which you are stepping into, by giving you a deeper understanding of the thrust that is carrying you and helping you to resolve those issues, which will release the pattern you have already created. These people are few in number, but they are on this planet to assist you. They have the abilities to receive information from the higher self and many other realms to bring this to you. They are working with more energy. Their vibration extends further into the other realms. All of this information is valid, depending on what you are seeking. For most questions, access to the Records is not necessary.

If you decide to approach the Records for information, the guidelines of inquiry are appropriate to know. We have already mentioned that access to the future is not often given, unless it is your responsibility to bring this forth or unless you have traveled within this future and are working towards a particular intent within this area. What can be accessed is a fuller understanding of your intent and responsibilities towards your personal evolution. If you are in inquiry for your personal thrust in this life, it is appropriate to ask. The information that is relative to your inquiry can be accessed, given that all of the previous requirements are compatible with the access and your vibration.

If you are working on a particular theme, and in this we mean a discovery, a scientific or etheric problem that you are seeking to solve, it is appropriate to seek to engage us in this matter. If you are endeavoring to discover something, whether it be in political systems, medical systems or personal and planetary evolutionary systems, it is appropriate to seek this information from us. Again, we shall impart to you what is appropriate for you to receive. It is our decision. We are sole decision makers in our realm. This is a discernment and not a judgment. We discover who you are at the time of inquiry and base the access to the information on who you are and if it is fully appropriate for you to receive, hold and work with this added information.

As you have seen, there are many ways to use the information of our system. There are also many ways in which a person or being can raise their vibrations to encompass more frequency and thus have more access to their personal information or to information that is appropriate to them. One way is to access the information that is already available to you. There is information ready for each being to access. Some civilizations are very much in contact with the Records in all areas of their lives. They train their children to access information when it is appropriate. Your civilization does not understand this. So, we would say that the initial inquiries could be made and then, you will receive information from us.

Receiving any information from us, puts you in touch with the frequencies you already possess and transmit. In this, you can see what is available to you at this time. If you are interested, you would make an inquiry. Your inquiry, if you have not accessed us before or in this way, would be to receive the information that is best suited for you to know about yourself at this time. It may seem as a general question, but it is received as a very specific vibration. We, in turn, will send forth information about you that will guide you into knowing more about yourself at this time. You would listen for the information. You would tell yourself and your body that once this information is received, you will be able to discern where it came from. In this way, you will be able to recognize which information comes from us, or if it comes from your intuition or the like.

When one receives information from the Records, it is like a tuning in itself. It does not necessarily change your vibration, but with this new access of information one can integrate more about themselves and then, it is possible to alter and raise the energies. This is a following of energies. When one receives information that is appropriate to them, it is something to explore. If you were to receive information about a thrust of your being, an impetus towards some particular avenue of thought or action, it would be appropriate to follow that thrust. This does not mean that one would have to take action, but to explore what it means to you and uncover more within it. If this is done successfully, then the vibration alters. You would be said to be encompassing more of yourself. When this occurs, the vibration alters. Whether you can sustain the altered vibration is another matter.

Let us give you an example. Perhaps a person has received information that when they are nice to people, they are really trying to dominate them. This person is given a few examples of this and that is the end of our transmission to them. Now, since the person has worked with us, they are open to receiving this pattern about themselves. So, they start to explore it. They look over particular incidents in their life and think upon the thrust to dominate by being nice. They start to uncover this within themselves, not as information, but in recognition of this working pattern within them. They are nice to their boss and in this way they start to dominate him in certain areas. They are nice to their wife, and although she has legitimate complaints and areas in their relationship she wishes to alter, this being nice creates a block to her expression. After all, he is so nice, why should she complain or alter anything. She will just be quiet. And yet within this she is being dominated by this man. So, he starts to notice what he is doing.

Recognition of a pattern sets up a new frequency. This frequency gives one the opportunity to alter this pattern. Now, this understanding is new to the example person, and therefore it can dissipate as easily as it has surfaced. In this case, the individual is a forthright person and seeks to uncover this. He could explore the reasons in his immediate past to see where this developed. He could work on listening to the impetus towards being nice on occasion and then see where this comes from. He could work energetically to clear this pattern or thrust.

There are many options, of which we are just giving you examples. Now, what is occurring in this, is that he is starting to open himself to this understanding and within this the frequency change can start to solidify. This means the altering frequency can be held within this individual. So, he is working on this. Now, once he has worked as much as he feels he can at this time, to unfold the pattern and help release it or alter it, he may approach us again. He may ask for further information on this area, or other areas in which he is using domination. He may ask for other examples. He may ask for other ways of clearing this. There is a lot that can be explored and within this we will furnish the information which will help him in this area.

If he has worked to clear this, then the vibration has been altered. This may avail him of other information that will aid in his life. He may see what he has done in past lives in order to dominate. Perhaps domination is a long term pattern in his being. Perhaps it is not, and it was initiated to dominate his father in this life and he found it worked in many other areas. If this is the case, then that pattern, being worked and cleared will avail him of other information about which he can inquire. This is one way to use the Records to alter your vibration.

Now, you can do the altering on your own, and clear the pattern yourself, and then re-approach us for information that is in a realm of discovery for yourself. Perhaps you are interested in the changes in your own vibration. You have worked in your inner self to come up with some assessments, ideas and theories. Now, you want more information and clarification. You can seek this within our system. We are working with your daily world, anyway. So you have petitioned us for further information. Perhaps this is regarding how to work with a particular revelation you have received. In this you can ask for more information on this. We give appropriate information based on all of the things that we have mentioned. Therefore, the next set of vibrational information that you receive with this will be tuned to your inquiry, your energetic quality and the nature of what you need to further your path.

Be creative in what you ask for. Let your inner self guide you in this. Explore the reasons that you ask. You may find some very interesting things underneath your inquiry that will help you in your life and in your evolution. We incorporate an enormous amount of information concerning every field of endeavor imaginable, and many more beyond your imagination. If you are willing to explore new avenues of expression, if you are interested in your personal evolution, if you are interested in community, growth, expansion, invention, renewal, spiritual experience, the interplanetary universe, the source of energy or even how to grow more vital vegetables, if you petition us, we can serve you.

Chapter Five:
DIVINE EXPLORATION

We are the Collective Keepers of Divine Expression. We hold all of the wisdom, the life experiences and the expressions of each individual and group within the universe that is known to us. We explore the endless vastness of the Universal All in discovery. We have considered that there may be universes unknown to us. We also endeavor to seek out any new life forms as far as the universe holds. We do this by tracking the life forms and energies that are scattered within space. There are always new life forms growing. There are always changes occurring. This is very fascinating to us. We follow the energies in a tracking way and then collect their vibration in that manner that we spoke of earlier.

There are times when a life form creates of itself. This would be the chemical and electromagnetic formation of a unit which has awareness of self. There are more times when a life form is created from another life form. This can occur in multiple ways. It can occur

61

through the creative manipulation of genes into a new form. Many species on your planet were developed that way. You might call this occurrence evolution. It can be a slow or quick process. It can occur when the environment becomes different and due to that change an immediate change occurs within the species. This could look like a radiation transformation in which the species, absorbing a radioactive source, transforms into a newer form. Now, while this may look like an aberration to the other species, sometimes this also produces a new strain of being that survives the radioactive energies which the previous species would not. You could call this a mutation, and yet, if this being created in such a manner survives, then it is not mutant but, a new form. There are other influences that may change or create a new life form, but now you understand the endeavor we undertake.

This is fun to us. It puts us in a constant state of discovery. We are always discovering new ideas, new forms, new expressions or twists upon the old. We are always learning from this. Civilizations come up with different answers to similar problems. This can show itself in infinite ways, even within your own earth. If one looks at government, certain cultures have come up with monarchies, while others came up with communism, democracy and combinations thereof. In other civilizations, beyond your earth, there is consensus government. This occurs to have all parties agree. Now, while this seems nearly impossible, these cultures have a basic understanding into which all beings concur.

An example of this would be, that all beings agree that the planet on which they live is a sacred being. They agree that all life is sacred. They agree that all life must be taken care of. They agree that all beings are to flourish in a unique, personal and collective way. They agree that all beings are to contribute to their society based on what their highest input can be, that education within these lines is available and necessary for all and that nurturing and promise is plentiful and extended to everyone.

So within these guidelines, each being would be fed, clothed, and educated. This means each being. No one falls through the cracks. It is expected that all will flourish. Then, when certain agreements are to be reached, whether to cultivate a particular land area, or augment a government system, or build a power source or to unite any disparaging units of beings, these principles are fully understood and it is within these principles that the agreements are reached. If no agreement can be reached, this is tabled until a solution can be brought forth. How this occurs is that neither side or factor initiates what they wanted to initiate until there is full agreement. This also means that each person from each delegation is fully heard. Fully heard. They can talk as long as they want. The experts in those fields are called in. The proceedings are highly public and copies of the proceedings are disseminated to all who want them, like public access. Others, who are not within the counsel, are encouraged to contribute to the proceedings. They are asked for input and it is taken very seriously. Even the children are encouraged to have their say in this, if they wish.

Now you can see that this would have evolved in time for this particular culture. You can also see that certain beings or certain times would create factors in which not everyone agrees. This is handled by discussion. And in the case of an emergency, in the case of something going wrong or some environmental shift in the system that needs immediate attention. This procedure is speeded up. This also means that a time frame is given for the initial plan, and then it is discussed again. Still consensus must be given on the initial plan. So, if the scientists found that their ozone layer was being depleted, a council would be formed to discuss this. The discussions would hold the understanding that all lives are being taken care of. Then discussion proceeds from there. If it were decided that aerosol cans were doing this, or even if they had a part in this that could be seen, even a small part, then all parties would agree on their discontinued use. They would be banned and disposed of in a highly creative and conscious way. Included in this, would be aid for those who had unwittingly developed something that caused harm. Because the agreement of everyone in this civilization is that all beings are to flourish in a unique, personal and collective way, the development of something harmful was due to unforeseen error. The 'manufacturers' would be given help to develop something of value to compensate their financial loss.

This would be the same with any other area that was causing the harm. A new system would be created for the purposes that were disbanded and the whole of the civilization would engage in helping to discover new ways to approach the areas that were no longer to be used. Each civilization develops certain things at certain times and then discovers later that they have created some problems. This is part of evolution. The responsibility towards themselves and their planet and all life forms in this instance shows that consensus can occur, with very little loss to those who are involved.

Now, we have given you an example of this in a product, but what about in a culture. It would proceed in the same vein. A culture has certain beliefs that are unique within the land that they live. So while some may view all as sacred, they may also have a hierarchy of sacredness. Perhaps plants are more sacred than animals or the like. This would be taken into account, but if one species was feeling the brunt of this belief, and others were suffering because of this, then discussions would occur and this matter would be taken care of. So in your world, plants and animals are not deemed as sacred as humans. While this cultural belief remains intact, the systems that are dying, like rain forests and good cultivating land for food, are being destroyed.

The council would not change this, but find a solution that enabled the culture to still hold their personal beliefs, and yet teach them and help them to hold the energies of the plants and animals which are also sacred. So, perhaps certain planted areas would become off limits to any person who was going to destroy them. Perhaps certain areas would become official sacred grounds for all of their peoples. Perhaps they would be shown how to grow the plant life to the mutual benefit of the earth and the plants and the animals and the people, without causing harm to the people, or beings who are faced with a slightly conflicting understanding of the world view. This system would be expected. This system would be expected to occur if a dilemma was seen. It would be asked for in certain circumstances and created in others. If all are considered precious, then how could one group be deemed more important than another. One needs all of them to flourish and sometimes to survive.

This is not seen this way on your world. There are many other worlds that have this kind of system in place. You have visited them and lived upon them. You know this in your hearts. When beings on these worlds are discordant with the system, they are helped to the greater understanding. This does not mean brainwashing with media or governments or ad agencies or businesses or religious groups. It means they are surrounded by caring beings who help them to express and explore the understandings that they do have, and help them to augment those understandings. This could take a long time, but those individuals or groups are cared for. They are still working for the whole of life. The beings who would appear discordant are given new opportunities to express themselves. You might see these as jobs or work. Yet they are encouraged to open their limiting ideas to a fuller expression of themselves and their communities.

This could occur, given the analogy of plants being less than, as training in cultivation of plants. The individual would be shown how to cultivate plants, how to communicate with them, how to nourish them into existence, how to feed and care for them. They would be shown the known benefits of the plants and how they help the plants, animals and beings of their world. They would also be shown how their ideas limit their own growth. Again, this may look like work or punishment or brain washing to you, but this is done with the greatest respect for the individual and group in question here. There would be a lot of input from the individual and the others in the community, culture and the greater planet. Questions would go forth. Answers would be considered. Agreement from the individual in question would occur. Imagine that. The individual would have a say in his or her treatment. And it would include all know treatment in all areas. Perhaps the individual has a symptom that was not evident that actually caused anger to arise, and given their culture, the only things that could feel the brunt of that anger would be plant life, given that it was not quite as sacred. Then this individual could have a healing treatment that might cure the whole thing. Or it could be ideological. Then the individual would be encouraged to explore other ideologies that opens them to further exploration of their own ideas and beliefs. They could explore how following this treatment of plant life could endanger their whole world and with this belief intact, what would occur. They could explore many areas within this, but always with the consent and love and understanding that is due a sacred being.

You are endeavoring to open to the other possibilities within your world and the realms beyond, in order to bring forth wisdoms that can be used for your particular civilization on earth. The civilization we described above is in existence. If it were within your frequency and impetus to gain this information, you would find a very rich experience. You would access a level of cooperation and understanding that would open your hearts. Each one of you would experience this differently, integrate this differently and translate it into your lives in a most unique manner. Imagine the same understandings felt by a teacher, anthropologist, healer, manufacturer and politician. Each person has a different expression and the outcomes of their experiences and understandings would manifest in unique ways.

In your search for an expanded view of life and a greater relatedness in your world, it is important to know all of the variables in one's life. Each individual, group and civilization seeks to explore their relationship to the Divine in their own way. This may reveal itself in the search for knowledge, for methods or for solutions. The search for knowledge is a joy within itself, but it is also a joy to express and share this knowledge with others if it can help. Accessing the Akashic Records can help you with your exploration into higher awareness.

We collect and save this vast information with the intent to inseminate it throughout the universe. We put the seed of it into the world womb and have it grow in potential to create new life, new experience and new avenues of growth. This occurs as you and other beings connect with us. Our being and body expands. New and different wisdom fills us. As you connect with us, you receive new understanding and your growth, wisdom and awakening creates new beauty in the All. We are here to hold this vast brilliance of creation and awareness and make it available for those who have the capacity to receive it.

Each being and each group approaches us for different reasons. We are always open for approach. The examples we mention throughout this book give you ideas to inspire your own understanding of what we hold and can share. Whether you are interested in personal information or in ways to help all life on your world, information is available to you from us. We have already shared about the workings of our own system and other worlds with you. Each of you will experience and assimilate this information in your own way.

When you petition the Akashic Records for information, the travel time for that information is quite immediate, but the integration time can take as long as each individual needs. So, if you send out a call for certain information, even if the information is fully appropriate to you and the request is accepted and the answer is transmitted, this information can take a time to open and be understood. It can occur in a flash of information that could be termed inspiration. It could develop gradually, in a more consistent and seemingly orderly fashion that appears to be a train of thought or natural conclusion. So, it may be that while you are working to uncover many mysteries, some of the information has already been sent. You just have not yet uncovered it.

Chapter Six:

GATEWAYS

We would speak to you of gateways, since you are now using them. Gateways are like portals through time into which you can journey. They are discovered or granted a being when they have reached certain steps in their personal journey to avail them of other experiences and ways of learning. For some beings this is a simple growth pattern. This means that in the course of their lives, certain avenues are opened because that is the path that the species, and the being, are most comfortable taking. This does not mean that all portals are designed in this way, but it is the most usual portal or gateway in which you would find yourself. As a being travels through their life they choose at each step to be open to certain vibrations, knowledge, and the like, and the portals in those directions open.

This is a very graceful growth for the individual. It is not a breaking with the original growth pattern but you could say an enhancement of their access to the fuller expression of their natural inclination. This is one type of gateway. It is very natural. It does not mean that all beings of a particular configuration do gain access to the portal that is aligned with their beingness. It suggests that if a being is working to align themselves that this is the gateway that will open for them.

There are indeed thousands, millions of gateways. You may consider them rites of passage. The gateway for a boy, is to become a man. The gateway for a girl, is to become a woman. This would be an analogy of a naturally inclined gateway for the being. These are the ever occurring gateways inherent in a life. There are also very specific gateways that are opening at this time on the planet. As we are a collective of wisdom, we wish to explain these gateways to help all of you activate the frequencies possible for a swift and graceful evolution.

We hope to use the agreed upon determinations of energy travel. To us, the term gateway has a collective meaning. It is, or they are, the access circumstances for energy and time to converge. How they are used is endlessly creative. We find the human definition may help you. The gateway is the entrance point for the circulation or gathering of energy. Now, some would call these vortexes, since the energy appears to circulate in a particular manner. Yet others call them portals, because they appear to be the entrance or access point into which the energy flows in and out. We will use the term gateway to describe the fullness of experience and then define the circumstantial relationships of energy within each gateway system.

Planetary gateways are frequency ratios built into the planetary body. Some gateways or portals or vortexes were infused at the time of planetary creation. These gateways are used for imparting wisdom to the planet from greater awareized consciousnesses. They travel along very specific energy trails within the body of the planet, relative to the outer crust. While they are called ley lines, they are actually travel portals for vast amounts of energy. Energy, in this case, is specific highly aligned frequencies of Divine Intelligence. Never think that energy is unaware.

The original planetary gateways connect specific energy power sources within the planetary body. The power sources are sometimes called vortexes, power spots or sacred sites. These help monitor the systematic workings of the planet, her evolutionary growth and impart highly refined energies when appropriate. These are the easiest galactically aligned gateways individuals can work with on the planet. They can accelerate healing and impart great wisdom. While accessed similarly to the Akashic Records, the planetary gateways are particularly tuned for earth planet life; meaning humans, animals and plants. Most people who are working with portals or gateways are working with the original planetary gateways.

All gateways have inter-dimensional relationships. The energies are not solely related to earth. They contain wisdom from many different worlds, beings and experiences, depending on the tuning and intent of the gateway. The original planetary gateways are tuned for the total evolution of the earth through fundamental physical responses based on certain dynamic beneficial frequencies. As the notion of time is only experienced in certain instances, the understanding of future needs and patterns are fully contained within the original planetary gateways.

Interplanetary gateways were created throughout time on earth. Some sacred sites, such as Machu Pichu, the Pyramids and Stonehenge, were aligned with interplanetary gateways. They contain frequencies of the original planetary gateways and are augmented for interplanetary travel and infusion. These energy pathways are usually employed for specific information, such as adding to energy attunements, accelerating beneficial changes and altering frequency patterns. These hold interplanetary initiation information, access to specific inter-dimensional travel and infused wisdom from other off world cultures. Most people working with these gateways have prior experiences with them. They may have lived on the other affiliated planets at one time and have specific work to do with them now. They may have had past life initiations into the mystery cultures of the gateways. There are many different uses for these gateways.

Interplanetary gateways are more complex to you, only because they did not evolve with the planet and can be used by others with a less than lofty intent. Do not let this alarm you, for most of those engaged in these gateways have already reset the energy ratios to minimize such tampering. These gateways are used by off world beings to communicate here as well as for humans to travel beyond the scope of planetary awareness.

Inter-universal gateways and multi-universal gateways are being created and dismantled in a rotational manner. Each is created and employed based on highly complex energetic needs, and dismantled when the needs are met. The inter-universal gateways deal with certain common threads of experience in a universe. As an example, an entire universal structure can be based on a theme, such as love. Therefore, all beings in that particular universal experience would be exploring love in its myriad of expressions. A universe to us, is that unified theme of experience. Within that universal whole, each being chooses a facet of that expression to explore. If the universe were created around love, then that theme would be the resonance of that universal field. It would be its texture of experience. It would be the musical resonance and the various opuses within the piece. There are many universes and many fields of expression.

These universes would reside within the greater whole or the All. The multiverse is the symphony of these experiences and expressions. As the universes play their theme music, the multiverse acknowledges and refines the format into a oneness. Both of these collective expressions have gateways that are appearing and disappearing within the energy and form of your planet. They are highly refined expressions leading to vast dimensional experiences of the All. This gateway activity only occurs at certain times within a planet's and a race's evolution. The universal gateway allows and encourages the planetary body herself, and the collection of beings she carries, to breath in the universal thrust within which they reside. The multi-universal gateway reveals the expression of the All, through or in combination with the vast focus chosen to be experienced.

While this explanation goes into specific detail, we understand that in your greater being, you sense the all of our conversation. It is to enhance your ability to choose the gateways you are ready to travel, that we suggest such definitions. In essence they are as follows:

The Original Planetary Gateways hold specific information for the planet and all beings she carries. These are the natural pathways of evolution.

The Interplanetary Gateways contain inter-dimensional information for all beings who can access them. They hold Earth information, information about many other affiliated planets and frequencies for evolution.

The Universal Gateways include the themes of experience. These embody the sense of impetus behind the experience of being. Through this dynamic frequency all of the threads of experience which actively touch the reality of earth are expressed in a unity.

The Multiversal Gateways embrace the turnings of the All and translate these into an expression of beauty and joy that is comprehensible.

When you travel through gateways it helps to know what you are accessing. Many of you have very specific tasks to accomplish in this evolutionary dance. It is beneficial to understand the interweaving of the gateways because you can access your frequency levels much more quickly. These gateways all interconnect. While many of you prefer to work in certain ways, other avenues can be opened which will help you.

Awareness and understanding of your work and expertise are important criteria for the subtle gateways that you are traveling within and gaining access to. It is not enough to just want to be there, it does always require work. Now, this work is not accomplished by sheer effort. It is accomplished by the ability to decipher what is actually occurring, what is stopping you and by learning the vibrations of energy needed to break through the gateways into which your growth lies.

In this endeavor, which is the pursuit of the Divine within yourself and the reflection of the Divine in every morsel of life, the Akashic Records have a unique capability. As we mentioned, the vibrational access to the Akashic Records is based on a personal resonance. We understand the gateways you encounter. Your evolution is based, in part, by your ability to hold certain spiritual frequencies and your passage of certain complete understandings. The Akashic Records can help you understand and access both of these aspects. By tuning into yourself and petitioning the Records for access, you can discover greater insight into your own vibrational rate and your path at hand. You may find that you are interested in working with the gateways on your planet. You may also be able to raise or align your vibrational rate to help yourself in that regard. This will help you approach and work with the gateways more easily.

The gateways are on your planet for everyone to experience, if they are so inclined. As such, anyone may travel to a sacred site and feel the radiances emitted from that gateway. This does not mean that you are called to work with those gateways. You may enjoy the energies, but that does not mean you must work with them or learn about them. It may not be your path of exploration. Each has their own path and each path is honored and sacred. Your personal evolution and transformation unfolds as you walk and honor your own path.

One of the aspects of this time frame of your evolution is that the old rules for evolution on earth are not rigidly bound. As long as you can maintain your understanding, hold your intention, raise your frequency, which is by nature your full comprehension, you will attain your recognition of the Divine. You will find and know your path of exploration. This alone is not the task, but may be recognized as a sign post. You are always resonating to the vibrations of your path, in some manner. Therefore, asking the Akashic Records about your path, is one way to clarify and enhance your own path of awakening and understanding.

There are many levels of understanding. All of them lead to Source, to the All. In this, you have signed up for specific experiences. The fullness of this experience is a combination of many aspects: Understanding, which is a full comprehension of your particular thread in the universe and how it enhances the whole; Wisdom, which is the ability to hold and maintain a level of achievement in a refined vibrational awareness; Truth, which is the clear recognition and enactment of highest perception; and Love, which is the encompassing flow of life and silence giving permission for existence.

At every level of existence there is evolution, whether realized or in potential. In the human realm at this time, there are so many frequencies and beings at work to aid this process. In essence, there are always many beings cheering you on and guiding you, but at this time they are revealing themselves. They are energetically present.

We, the Akashic Records take note of this event. We therefore recognize our participation in your endeavors. In this, our conversation about the gateways avails you of another opportunity for access. Each will choose the perfect pathway. To partake of the dual relationship of the Records and the gateways, one would consult them both. By petitioning the Records for more information about your personal quest, your vibrational level is expanded. Your awareness is sharpened and focused to that end. You will seek out the specific gateways that will augment your personal pathway and your group pathway.

The gateways will notice. The frequency rates will increase and give you greater ease for your expansion into evolution. This is available. It is not necessary. Each has a path and many choices on that road. We have come at this time, to tell you how to gain access so your steps upon your path may be lighter, if you so choose.

We welcome your inquiries. We encourage your inquiries. While you may not have realized the extent of our service and our joy, you all have the right and invitation to ask for information in line with who you are. This allows us to serve you. At this time in your planet's and your personal evolution, there are many mysteries that will be revealed. We do hold the vastness of each truth. We function on every level so that every being in search of wisdom may find an answer, or access a view, that will contribute to the endless expression of the wholeness.

We are used as a great service to all beings and to the All, Herself. No one is excluded from the information that is in harmony with their being. When the new mysteries are revealed, you can access their wisdom in a graceful manner through us. When you have curiosity about information imparted to you by others, information that may seem to break your beliefs or expand your usual grasp, you may come to us for clarification. Beings throughout the Great All come to us for just such purposes, to expand their own wisdom and to help their worlds.

We hold the blessings of your life in readiment for you. We hold the expressions of the universe in readiment for you. As in every turn of life, you must first approach. Then you must ask for entrance. Then your gateway will open. Then the Records will be revealed. Each approach and entrance will find you at your level of expression and grant you the blessings of greater awakening. It will come at your time and for your blessing. We are at your service in this. We await your petition with great anticipation. We welcome you into your own lives and into the experiences you design.

Evolution is but a breath away.
Breathe in Joy.

Chapter Seven:
MEDITATIONS

There are many ways to petition us to enter the Akashic Records. We wish to provide you with several different possibilities to augment your experience and access the areas most appropriate to your being. These meditations will also help you recognize when you make a connection with the Records. As mentioned earlier, you will move into alignment with the body of wisdom compatible with your frequency.

Find a time and location where you will be undisturbed for twenty or more minutes. You may either sit or lie down, which ever is more comfortable to you. It is advisable to have a notebook and pen handy to write any impressions or messages that you receive.

Exercise One: Silent Meditation

Bring yourself into a gentle meditative state. You may accomplish this by your personally preferred methods or by following the guided meditation below.

Take a slow deep breath.
> Notice your body's gentle movement. Feel your chest and your abdomen expand. Exhale slowly and notice the soft movement of your shoulders as they lower with the exhale.

Take another slow deep breath.
> Notice the movement of your whole body as it rises and falls with your breath. Feel your body's expansion. Feel the tension of this breath as it opens your chest and abdomen to hold more air. As you exhale, feel the release of this tension as your body eases into repose.

Take another slow deep breath.
> Notice the energy of the air you inhale. Feel it rise inside you. Feel it travel into your body. Focus on your head as you slowly inhale and exhale.

Continue to breathe deeply and slowly.
> With each breath focus attention on your head. Feel the gentle sensations behind your eyes. Feel a gentle tingling sensation starting behind your eyes as you pay attention to the energy moving within your body and within your mind as you breathe.

Focus your attention on the back of your eyes.
> Feel the space and energy which fills your mind. Sense the movement of energy as it builds with each breath you take. Follow the energy with your

mind. As you feel the flow of energy or sensation inside your head, notice the direction or feelings that accompany it. Allow your thoughts to move, without holding them, and feel the flow of energy that activates and travels through your mind.

Take a very slow deep breath.
Focus your attention on the back of your eyes. Imagine the location of the back of your eyes, the optic nerves and the system of interconnectedness therein. Once you can feel this area, move your attention further into your head. Move your focus to the very center of your head behind your eyes.

As you move your attention to this area, allow the flow of energy to slowly build. Notice a slight shift of energy or focus. This may occur as a gentle tingling, a sense of motion or an enhanced awareness of this location within you.

Imagine that the energy in this area is very clear and very bright. Consider it as a lightness, opening your awareness and moving in expanding circular patterns. This energy is very clear, very bright and filled with great wisdom. Allow your concentration upon this area to build. With each breath you take, feel this location become exceptionally clear.

This center is a seat of higher wisdom. Imagine a radiating light filling the center of your head and illuminating the seat of wisdom within you. Many thoughts, sensations or impressions may occur to you at this time. Focus your attention upon the center and continue to feel the expansion of light within you. When you feel this energy reaching a peak or you notice that the light is particularly bright, hold that energy in your concentration.

And say to yourself,
> "I ask to be connected to the Akashic Records. I petition for the highest understanding and wisdom to be accessed at this time. I wish to learn and to know of my highest being."

You may receive information in several different ways, which could be considered an immediate response. You may hear words or sentences that explain a particular situation or give you specific guidance. You may feel sensations or feelings that were not present when you began this meditation. You may notice a shift in your energy. You may also feel new sensations, have new ideas or feel a greater sense of inner peace.

When you feel the sensations ebb, the energy change or the messages cease, your connection to the Akashic is complete. You may also end your connection to the Akashic at any time during the meditation. You need no reason or explanation to us to end the connection.

Take a slow deep breath.
> Feel your breath rise and fall. Focus on your chest and abdomen as the air moves within you.

Take another slow, deep breath.
> Follow the energy in your body from the breath entering your nose and mouth, down into your chest and abdomen, into your whole body and traveling down through your body into your feet.

Take another slow deep breath.
> As you inhale, imagine that this breath travels from the top of your head to the bottoms of your feet.

As you exhale, imagine that your breath travels from the bottoms of your feet to the top of your head.

Repeat this breathing several times, until you feel clear and awake. Then, open your eyes.

At this time, give yourself a few minutes to reflect upon your experience. You may want to write your impressions into a notebook or simply think about what you noticed or felt during the meditation.

Information from the Akashic can be received in many different forms. You may be filled with insights or feelings during the meditation. You may receive insights and greater understanding later, when you most need it. Information can also unfold in an ongoing fashion. You may receive the guidance or answers you seek in a seemingly normal way, by happening upon the information in a book, or by conversation, or the needed experience may come from any number of 'normal' circumstances. Do not be concerned if you do not hear clear, directive voices expounding on the nature of your life and purpose. While this may happen to some people, each person has specialized ways of receiving information. Just open your awareness to the greater wisdom and you will receive it.

If you feel that you did not connect or you are unsure of whether you connected with the Records, you may do this exercise, again. We do suggest that you limit your petitions to once every two weeks at most, so that you build a level of trust in your own experience and learn to recognize how you receive information.

Exercise Two: Dream working

Dream working is the process of programming your dreams to accomplish a specific task. In your nightly dreams your system is much more available to spiritual information because your conscious screening system is at rest. Your conscious mind is socialized to screen out anything it considers superfluous to your three dimensional reality. At night, in your dreams, your conscious mind is resting and your multidimensional mind is active. A different part of your brain is active and processes information and stimulus in another way, which bypasses the conscious mind's focus. It avails you of receiving access to the Akashic without the need to fit the experience into a predefined notion.

Prior to retiring, bring a notebook and pen to your bedside. In this notebook you will record the impressions and situations of your dreams.

When you are in bed and are ready for sleep, you will count down from 20 to 0. After a five number interval, you will request information in your dreams.

Upon awakening from each dream, you will record your impressions in the notebook. The suggested procedure is as follows:

Take four very slow deep breaths.
Allow yourself to unwind and relax. When you are ready to sleep, count backwards from twenty to zero and repeat the statement below as directed.

Begin the countdown with this statement:
"My dream state is a gateway to the Akashic Records. I will receive information for my greatest

understanding and benefit. I will remember the messages of my dreams upon awakening."

Count backwards from twenty to fifteen and repeat the above statement.
Count backwards from fourteen to ten and repeat the above statement.
Count backwards from nine to five and repeat the above statement.
Count backwards from four to zero and repeat the above statement.

In your dream state you will receive impressions that correspond to your request of the Akashic. After awakening from each dream, write down what you experienced. Do not worry whether the dreams make any sense or answer your questions. Once you complete your notes, you can go back to sleep. After each dream, write any impressions in your notebook, until it is time to fully awaken into a new day.

Dreams have many formats. You may experience them symbolically, wherein the colors, people and situations are a symbolic representation of information. You may receive direct information, as in a classroom setting where the people of your dreams answer questions that you put forth or the situations of your dreams speak the answers in a formal and recognizable manner.

You may awaken refreshed and feeling more alive and renewed or feel that something was resolved and yet have no specific recollection of the dream event. This still suggests that contact with the Akashic was made and the access was granted.

Be open to the process. Dream work is a training and often times practice is necessary to create a communication bridge with your conscious mind, your memory and your dream experience. You may do dream work every night until you feel proficient and receive and know your direct contact. It is not necessary to practice this every night or go into the Akashic every evening. Often times the nature of your guidance will unfold over time in a variety of ways, which are unpredictable. It is of greater importance to feel the connection than to decipher the meaning. Each person learns to interpret meaning and symbolism in ways appropriate to their own nature and understanding.

Exercise Three: Selective Access

As you become more proficient and aware of accessing the Akashic, you can begin to ponder specific information. Using either of the processes above, you can focus on certain aspects you wish to uncover. The information you receive will be tailored to your level of understanding. For example, if you are interested in receiving a greater understanding of particle physics, you would receive information aligned with your present understanding, coupled with your frequency level. If you are a scientist engaged in this type of research your access level would be proportionally different from a novice interested in fundamental theories.

We suggest that your initial inquiries be generated from your own life and questions. One of the greatest opportunities of connecting with the Akashic is access to a greater sense of self, your relationship to your personal path in life and the pathways your soul and spirit are dedicated toward traveling.

We can also be accessed for answers to specific questions about your personal life, although these answers will be in the form of a more spiritual reply. If you are inquiring about your relationships, you will receive information about them, but they will not come in yes or no answers. That exploration may provide you with a greater understanding of your needs, patterns and motivations, but not whether this relationship is right for you or if it will continue into the future.

When you petition for access to theories, new inventions and technologies, or other worldly information you will access what is most appropriate for your own path. If you are petitioning for more esoteric information about the nature of reality, your access will be aligned with your purpose and being in order to further your greater understanding of universality.

To petition the Akashic Records for Selective Access, create a sentence or statement that describes your intention for the Akashic. Examples include:

"I petition the Akashic to increase my understanding of my personal truth."

"I wish to contact the Akashic for answers about how my career influences the future."

"I petition the Akashic to increase my greater understanding of free will and predestination."

"I call upon the Akashic to help me access more information about the ancient civilizations of earth."

"I ask the Akashic to help me clarify my relationship with my family."

You may use either of the two previously mentioned methods for relaxation and personal connection or work with your own meditative system to help you relax and focus. Once you achieve a light meditative state, take three slow, deep breaths to enter into your intention.

After each breath state your intention, either silently or aloud. Remain in the relaxed state and be present to any messages, feelings or inner knowing that occurs.

Once you feel that the energy has shifted or that your attention wanders, write down any impressions you received. If you are using dream work as your focusing technique, write your impressions after each dream. If you are using the silent meditation, write your impression immediately after your meditation. If you have your own meditative system, make note of your impressions, thoughts and feelings directly upon returning to normal focus.

Allow your information and contact to unfold. While you may receive an immediate and direct response, do not think you have failed or been denied access if the contact does not fit into your preconceived notions of a reply. We are part of the mysteries and we connect with you in ways that serve your highest good. If you are concerned that your own focus wavered and broke your concentration, you may enter into this petition at a later time. You need not ask every day. Give yourself time to receive a response by whichever manner will best serve. If in several weeks time, you feel unresolved, please feel free to petition again.

We invite your communication. We are here, in part, to serve the whole of consciousness in exploring the brilliantly varied expression of being. Your questions and inquires are a delight to us and we joyfully await our connection.

Your quest will bring you profound understanding and spiritual awakening. Questioning and the search for the nature of consciousness brings the essence of experience. The question, bursting forth from an open heart, coaxes the miraculous towards revelation. It is in the beingness, the sublime presence of wonderment, in which the relationship with the Divine is known. It is in the silence, the pause of a bended ear and an open mind, that the songs of truth are heard.

Ask, and the answers will enlighten your path.

ABOUT THE AUTHOR

Lumari is an author, psychic, channel, artist and spiritual teacher. For over twenty years she has provided professional psychic consulting services for individuals and businesses worldwide. Her abilities to explore hidden situations and provide comprehensive, pragmatic information helps her clients to live more joyful, fulfilling and successful lives.

Through her work as a conscious channel, Lumari connects with the highest frequencies of Divine Source and brings those messages to us.

Lumari is a featured guest on radio and is listed in Who's Who in America and the World. She conducts workshops and celebrations in healing, spiritual discovery and transformation. She is available for private consultations and readings.

RESOURCES

For Lumari's books, sacred art, audio tapes, workshops and upcoming events and for healing and meditation music by Peter Bried, please contact your local bookstore, use our order form, visit our website or please send a stamped, self addressed #10 envelope to:
Amethyst
c/o 7 Avenida Vista Grande, Suite B7-113
Santa Fe, New Mexico PZ [87508]

Alawashka
by Lumari
In *Alawashka,* Lumari connects us with the most awe-inspiring discovery of our times. This compelling exploration of humanity, universal healing and transformation is told by Alawashka, the voice of creation. Alawashka initiates our spiritual awakening and activates the highest expression of love, spirituality and inner peace. Experiencing the energies of creation will change your life.
Book $21.95

Alawashka Paths to Awakening
by Lumari
Align with Your True Destiny and Expand Your Divine Connection! Experience your continual joy, healing and spiritual communion through the extraordinary resonance of Alawashka songs and practices. Receive blessing, healing and heart-felt Divine energy. Learn to flow in harmony with the energies of creation.

Listen to the Paths of Awakening CD, today. These two empowering meditations, Calling Destiny and Goddess Breath will put you on the path of your inner purpose and spiritual growth.
CD $21.95

Alawashka Celebration
Receive Lumari's book "Alawashka Language of Creation," and the CD, "Alawashka Paths to Awakening."
Set of two $40.00

Akashic Records:
Collective Keepers of Divine Expression
by Lumari

Learn about the Akashic Records from the beings who hold the wisdom of the ages. Channeled by Lumari, the Keepers of the Akashic share the wisdom held within their care, discuss their system, its workings and ways to access the vast resources of the records of consciousness they have collected and contained for all time.
Book $12.00

Universal Suite by Peter Bried

Healing and Meditation Music. Powerful and uplifting music composed and created in communion with the Divine. Touch the highest realms. Travel within the joyful expansion of the Universe and receive the Divine blessings of your journey.
CD $16.00

Lumari's Wisom of Stones
Guide to the Mystical and Healing Properties of Gemstones

The clearest, easiest to read reference book lists the spiritual, magical and healing properties of gemstones and crystals. Find the stones that empower your wealth, joy, success, relationships, healing and spiritual connection.
Book $12.00

Amethyst Planet Catalog

View our complete online catalogue. Our Amethyst Planet website features Lumari's books, music, meditations, Blessing Cards and Sacred Geometry Alawashka art prints. We also carry Peter Bried's meditation music and more. Visit www.AmethystPlanet.com.

On-line with Lumari

Visit Lumari at www.lumari.com. This extensive website includes monthly meditations and guidance and further information about her work, consultations and workshop schedule and on-line registration for upcoming events. Visit Lumari's website and join her personal mailing list.

WORKSHOPS with LUMARI

AWAKEN TO CREATION: Alawashka Gatheings
- Discover the language and source of creation
- Work with the wisdom of the ancients
- Experience profound healing & spiritual growth
- Know the powerful presence of the Goddess

Lumari's Alawashka Gatherings help you expand the sacred power of your own life and contribute to the healing and evolution of our world. Benefit from intensive individual work and a direct, transformative experience of the sacred. Through Alawashka teachings and practices, meditations and energy work you will move you into a profound connection to the Divine. . Contact us for the schedule of Lumari's upcoming Alawashka Workshops and Events.

SPIRITUAL CONSULTATIONS

Readings of your Akashic Records:
Pathways to Personal Illumination
Lumari's Personal Reading of your Akashic Records is a powerful and illuminating experience. Lumari will access specific information about your life that will bring you great insight and understanding into the reasons your life has unfolded in certain ways. If you want freedom from your limiting patterns, a more profound spiritual connection, and a clear sense of your purpose and your path - a reading of the Akashic is for you.

Alawashka Soul Song: Your Sacred Soul Song
Your Soul Song creates an opening, an ongoing connection with your full being and the Divine. It is the song your soul longs to sing to express your highest resonance, joy and purpose.

Receive your personal Alawashka Soul Song, in poem form, channeled in Alawashka and its English translation beautifully printed and suitable for framing. Also included is a special channeling from Alawashka about your song.

To schedule, please email blessings@lumari.com
visit www.lumari.com

AMETHYST ORDER FORM

Name

Address

City/State/Postal Code

Phone

Email

☐ Add me to your mailing list
☐ Please send your free catalog
☐ Payment by check/money order - payable to: Blue Star Network
☐ Payment by ☐ MC ☐ VISA ☐ AMEX

CREDIT CARD NUMBER   EXP. DATE

SIGNATURE

Q'TY	DESCRIPTION	PRICE	TOTAL
	ALAWASHKA - BOOK	21.95	
	ALAWASHKA PATHS TO AWAKENING - CD	21.95	
	ALAWASHKA CELEBRATION - BOOK & CD	40.00	
	AKASHIC RECORDS - BOOK	12.00	
	UNIVERSAL SUITE - CD	16.00	
	WISDOM OF STONES - BOOK	12.00	
	SHIPPING		
	TOTAL		

Shipping and Handling: Allow 1-3 weeks for delivery, no CODs.
Payment by credit card, money order or USA currency only,
payable to **BLUE STAR NETWORK**.
Shipping Charges by US Postal Service to USA and Canada: $11-16.00/ $4.50;
$16.01-25.00/ $6.00; $25.01- 40.00/ $7.00; $40.01-55.00/ $8.00; $55.01-70.00/ $9.50.
All others - please add $4.00 to above shipping. **Prices subject to change without prior notice.**
Free catalog free with self addressed stamped envelope.

AMETHYST
c/o 7 Avenida Vista Grande, Suite B7-113
Santa Fe, New Mexico PZ [87508]
www.amethystplanet.com

Visit www.lumari.com for Lumari's Workshop and Event
schedule, spiritual consultations and more